RMS TITANIC

The Story Illustrated With Postcards of the Period

by R. Fletcher

RMS TITANIC

The story illustrated with postcards of the period

by R. Fletcher

Published by:

R. Fletcher

P. O. Box 42, Rugby, Warks. CV23 9AR, UK

ISBN 0-9540890-0-6

Printed by:

RCS Plc,

Randall Park Way, Retford DN22 7WF, UK.

CONTENTS

INTRODUCTION

In the late 20th Century the modern passenger aircraft have ended the reign of the great trans-Atlantic liners, but at the beginning of the century it was very different.

The White Star Line was one of the companies competing for the lucrative transatlantic trade. In response to strong competition from liners of The Hamburg-Amerika Line, the blue riband liners of Cunard and others, The White Star Line decided to build 2 Great liners with a third added later. These were the Olympic, Titanic, and Gigantic (later renamed Britannic). It was the loss of the Titanic in 1912 which still captures the imagination today nearly 90 years later, as it did in 1912. Following the discovery by Robert Ballard of the wreck on the sea bed, and the highly successful James Cameron film, interest has never been so high.

Using old postcards from the era, the aim of this book is to illustrate the disaster of the Titanic from her conception through to her sinking and the aftermath of the disaster. These postcards were produced during the 'Golden age' of collecting postcards, which declined during the middle of the century becoming popular again because of their beauty and the images they contain.

Titanic postcards have become highly sought after, with the rare and pre-sinking and photographic cards attracting a premium. Many cards were produced after the sinking showing a variety of related subjects, and as Titanic photographs were not readily available, many photographs and paintings of the Olympic (labelled as Titanic) were used.

This book does not show all Titanic postcards available but an example of postcards collectors may find for their collections. It also shows you how to tell the difference between Olympic and Titanic and gives a GENERAL GUIDE to their valuation.

I hope you enjoy this journey through some of the Titanic, and related, postcards available, and the stories they contain.

For Paula, Alex and Christopher (Hopper).

RMS LUSITANIA

(Colour postcard published by Morris & Co. Liverpool)

The story really begins in 1906 when two Cunard ships were launched. The first was the ill-fated RMS Lusitania, length 790 feet 32,000 tons.

The ship regained the Blue Riband for the fastest Atlantic crossing in 1907 and was later to be sunk without warning by a German U-boat in 1915.

The ship was powered by the new steam turbines driving quadruple screws, with slim lines built for speed, but with real luxury.

SS MAURETANIA

(Published FGO Stuart #2113)

RMS Mauretania was the second ship launched. Slightly longer and heavier than Lusitania, she was faster and a healthy rivalry between the two ships for the Blue Riband existed for many years.

With the success of Lusitania and Mauretania, White Star decided in 1907 to build two 45,000 ton Olympic class liners (later to become three liners), fifty percent larger and almost 100 feet longer than the Cunard vessels.

Based on their policy of comfort rather than speed, the liners would combine the utmost luxury, stability and reliability of service.

RMS LAURENTIC

(Colour postcard published by Tuck, 'Celebrated liner' series #9503)

The engines for the new White Star liners consisted of two reciprocating engines and a low pressure steam turbine driven from exhaust steam, driving two outer propellers and one centre propeller.

It had been found that this engine arrangement in the Laurentic showed an outstanding increase in economy and efficiency when compared with the identical but conventionally powered Megantic.

With lower vibration, higher economy, but slightly slower speed, it would allow for a transatlantic crossing time of just a week.

RMS OLYMPIC

(Published by Kingsway, UK)

RMS Olympic was to be the first of the Olympic class of ships built. The keel of the ship was laid in December 1908 and she was launched in October 1910.

After the launch her 29 huge boilers were fitted and then she was moved into the Thompson outfitting wharf. She was completed just over seven months later in May 1911.

RMS TITANIC

(Published by Beagles & Co. using Central News photograph, and it is a genuine photograph of Titanic as she leaves Southampton - Price band A)[1]

Titanic was the second of the Olympic class vessels. The keel was laid in March 1909 and she was launched May 1911, witnessed by more than 100,000 people.

Her first sea trials were delayed until April 2nd 1912 by bad weather. All the small delays in the Titanic completion would lead to the eventual collision with the iceberg.

Had the liner been a few hours or a day early the disaster may never have happened.

---

[1] As an aid to the date of publishing, a postally used postcard like the illustration above is very useful. This particular example was postally used April 25th 1912, very shortly after the disaster.

RMS BRITANNIC

(Publisher Signal, showing the Britannic nearing completion - Price band B)

The third of the Olympic class vessels was ordered in 1911. Originally named Gigantic this was changed (after the sinking of Titanic) to the Britannic. Launched February 1914, she was completed December 1915[2].

Britannic postcards are more difficult to find or collect than the other sister ships, as she never entered passenger service and consequently not many postcards were produced.

[2] She too was to meet a tragic end. With war in Europe raging she was immediately put into service as a hospital ship. It was during November 1916 that she struck a mine in the Aegean Sea, and sank within an hour.

THE GANTRY AT HARLAND & WOLFF

(Published by W, UK. Just visible in the centre of the postcard is the just laid keel of the Olympic - Price band A)

Harland & Wolff had previously built many liners for the White Star line, and was chosen to build the Olympic class vessels.

These were to be the largest vessels ever built and to accommodate their construction, three existing berths were converted into two. Enclosing the construction was a specially built 200 foot high, 840 feet long and 270 feet wide steel gantry.

The two ships were to be built side by side with the Olympic's construction a few months ahead of the Titanic.

SHIPBUILDING YARD, BELFAST

(Sepia tinted card showing stern view of Olympic and Titanic side by side under construction. WR & S Reliable Series - Price band B)

The gantry was erected to carry the cranes (capable of lifting between three and ten tons) necessary for economic erection and hydraulic riveting of the vessels.

Connected by girders, with solid concrete foundations resting on 40 foot piles, it carried four large electric lifts, two inclined walkways, and weighed nearly 6000 tons[3].

[3] Titanic/Olympic/Britannic were the only giant liners to be built using the Gantry at Harland & Wolff.

HARLAND & WOLFF, BELFAST

(Colour card showing bow view of Olympic and Titanic side by side under construction. Philco Series - Price band B)

The liners had a total of 8 decks plus an orlop deck at each end, 2 expansion joints to relieve stresses at sea and all exposed decks sheathed in wood.

Constructed of mild steel plate on a mild steel frame with 15 watertight bulkheads all held together by rivets up to 1 ½" in diameter.

The view of the vessels as they neared completion must have been an impressive sight for the 14000 workers of Harland & Wolff as they made their way to work.

QUEEN'S ISLAND SHIPYARDS

(Publisher unknown. Visible in the gantry the hull of Titanic, under construction, with most of the superstructure completed - Price band C)

The Titanic was built to the greatest standards of the day. Hydraulically riveted (about three million rivets weighing approx. 1200 tons), quality mild steel plates, six feet wide and about thirty feet long, and a double bottom.

It had a solid cast rudder built in 5 sections, twenty-nine 15' 9" diameter boilers, 2 sets of four cylinder triple expansion reciprocating engines, refrigeration unit for the latest in cold storage, and all of this made for an impressive specification.

THE TITANIC'S LAUNCH

(Published by J. Johnson Belfast - Price band C+)

Final preparations were complete, the hydraulic launch triggers, wooden bow launching cradle and temporary viewing platform (for the dignitaries) in place, the shores and blocks were removed.

At 12:13 on May 31st 1911, with Lord Pirrie (the Harland & Wolff chairman), J.Pierpont Morgan, and Bruce Ismay plus a viewing public of over 100,000 the great liner was launched.

THE TITANIC'S LAUNCH

LAUNCH OF THE GIANT WHITE STAR LINER "TITANIC" 45,000 TONS. BELFAST. MAY 31st, 1911.
LARGEST VESSEL IN THE WORLD.

(Published by Walton, Belfast, The Real Photo Series - Price band C)

It required twenty-two tons of tallow, train oil and soap an inch thick to grease the slipways.

Three anchors placed each side on the river bed and eighty tons of cable drag were used to stop the hull after she had hit the water.

The complete journey down the slipway took 62 seconds[4].

[4] The successful launch was marred by the death of a worker (James Dobbins 43). Injured removing a wooden support, he later died of his injuries in hospital.

THE TITANIC'S LAUNCH

(Published by Walton, Belfast. Visible on the front of the ship is the wooden launch cradle - Price band D)

Above postcard shows the Titanic at rest in the river Lagan.

After removal of the metal hawsers from the riverbed anchors, and the drag chains, the vessel was towed by tugs to her berth for fitting out.

On the same day Harland & Wolff officially handed over the Olympic to The White Star Line. Later Morgan, Ismay and other assembled dignitaries sailed back to Liverpool aboard the Olympic.

THE CENTRE ANCHOR OF TITANIC

(Published by J. P. & S. B. The postcard shows the nearly 17 ton anchor prior to its journey to Belfast - Price band D)

The size of the new vessels meant that the usual two 7 ¾ ton side bower anchors would have to be supplemented with a giant nearly 17 ton centre anchor. The cables needed to raise and lower all the three anchors had a length of 330 fathoms and weighed over 96 tons. It was manufactured by Messrs. N.Hingley & Sons, Dudley.

The wire hawser used with the centre anchor was 9 ½" circumference and 175 fathoms long and was supplied by Messrs. Bullivant & Co Ltd., London and was guaranteed to withstand a breaking strain of 280 tons. A team of twenty horses would be used to pull the 17 ton anchor to the railway station for the journey to Belfast.

FITTING OUT TITANIC

THE TITANIC—In the Ship Yards at Belfast, Ireland

(USA Published by Raphael & Co. Chicago from a set of 12 - Price band B)

The cable links for the centre anchor were welded on one side, three links in five feet. The cable links were 5 ¾" and 6 ¼" diameter and these were some of the largest links ever made.

The chains, specially forged by N. Hingley & Sons Ltd, were used to raise and lower the 17 ton anchor. Each link was made before being moved on, by hand, to allow for the next link to be added.

Because of the large size of the links most of this work was completed outside and required up to 5 big strong men to handle the large cable links.

FITTING OUT THE TITANIC

(Publisher unknown - Price band D)

Titanic was built to the highest standards of the day and the rare postcard above shows the liner being fitted out.

WHITE STAR OFFICES - LIVERPOOL

(Publisher unknown - Price band A)

Photograph of the White Star offices in Liverpool. White Star was partially owned by USA Financier J.P.Morgan and the company President Bruce Ismay.

BUILDERS OF THE TITANIC AND OLYMPIC

(Published by Walton, Belfast - Price band C)

Just some of the 19000 men employed by Harland and Wolff to build the Olympic and Titanic.

In the background the hull of the Titanic.

INTERIOR OF THE TITANIC AND OLYMPIC

(Colour postcard publisher unknown - Price band A)

Few postcards of the interior of the Titanic exist.

The following postcards of the Olympic's interior, although not exactly the same, give some indication of what the Titanic's passengers would have been accustomed to.

The caption on the reverse of the postcard reads:
'The Verandah Café looks out across the water, bright in the sunshine or deep blue under the stars. In this attractive spot, with the tang of the salt in the air, passengers may enjoy many an hour of content and good fellowship, over an aperitif or a cup of tea'.

INTERIOR OF THE TITANIC AND OLYMPIC

(Published by C.R. Hoffmann, Southampton #1155 - Price band A)

The 1st class smoking room was the finest of its kind, 65ft long, 63ft wide and 12ft 3in high. Constructed in the Georgian style, and based on the decorations of old English houses of the 1700's.

Mahogany carved walls inlaid with mother-of-pearl, with a large open fireplace. The windows were painted with landscapes, ships and other subjects.

INTERIOR OF THE TITANIC AND OLYMPIC

(Published by C.R. Hoffmann, Southampton #1171 - Price band A)

The first class restaurant, 60 ft long by 45ft wide, was decorated in the Louis XVI period. It was panelled in French walnut, carved and gilded, brass and gilt candle lamp holders, an elegant Axminster pile carpet and a bandstand at either end.

Tables and chairs with Aubusson tapestry upholstery, arranged to seat from two to eight people.

INTERIOR OF THE TITANIC AND OLYMPIC

Main Salon of the Ill Fated Titanic

(Published by Raphael & Co. Chicago, USA from a set of 12 - Price band B)

The first class Dining Saloon, 114ft long and the whole width of the ship (92 ft), was the largest afloat.

Decorated in the Jacobean style, it was painted white with a richly moulded ceiling. The floor was linoleum tiled and oak furniture with provision for 532 passengers to dine at the same time.

THE HMS HAWKE INCIDENT

(Published by Silk, Portsmouth - Price band B)

It was at the start of Olympic's fifth voyage to New York, under the command of Captain E. J. Smith, that a collision occurred with the Royal Navy ship HMS Hawke. It was when HMS Hawke was steaming parallel to the Olympic that she was sucked into the stern section holing the liner[5].

Fortunately nobody was hurt in the incident and both vessels limped back to port. The subsequent inquiry found the Olympic to blame.

[5] A large vessel moving at speed through water displaces water at the bow, radiates it out in the middle and sucks it back in at the stern.

THE HMS HAWKE INCIDENT

(Publisher unknown, visible in the postcard the forty foot long gash that resulted from the collision - Price band B)

The repairs necessary diverted workers from the Titanic and this caused White Star to reschedule the maiden voyage date.

2 SISTERS TOGETHER

(Publisher Walton, Belfast - Price band C)

This postcard shows one of the very few times the 2 sister ships were photographed together.

In February 1912 Olympic returned to Belfast after losing a propeller while crossing the Atlantic. The Titanic was taken out of the dry dock[6] where she was being completed and the Olympic was repaired.

This contributed to the delay in completing the Titanic, pushing back the maiden voyage date still further.

[6] The only dock big enough to fit the new liners was at Belfast

TITANIC SEA TRIALS

THE S. S. "TITANIC",
FOUNDERED APRIL 15TH 1912, ON HER ILL-FATED MAIDEN VOYAGE TO NEW YORK,
ONLY 705 BEING SAVED OUT OF A TOTAL OF 2,358 PASSENGERS AND CREW.

(Published by Hurst & Co. Belfast, The Real Photo Series. The postcard shows the Titanic preparing for her sea trials on April 1st - Price band B)

The sea trials were delayed till April 2nd due to bad weather. Smoke can be seen coming from her three forward funnels as the fourth funnel was for ventilation and it was thought to improve the aesthetic appearance of the vessel.

In the background the new 150 ton floating crane can be seen. This was used to lift the large and heavy engines, boilers, funnels etc.

TITANIC SEA TRIALS

(Austrian postcard, published by Bruder Kohn, Wien. The postcard shows Titanic leaving Belfast - Price band B)

The sea trials consisted of testing all the machinery, including the steering gear, and a series of runs at different propeller rpm to relate her performance to engine room indications.

Also tested was her ability to stop in an emergency. The ship was set to 20 knots and the engines thrown into full power reverse. The result was a stopping distance of just under half a mile.

FAREWELL TO BELFAST

(Published by Hurst & Co. the photograph used was of the Olympic but was titled the Titanic leaving Belfast - Price band B)

At the end of the sea trials the Titanic's official certificate of seaworthiness was handed over, and under the command of Captain Smith, she set sail for Southampton, arriving just before midnight on April 3rd.

FAREWELL TO BELFAST

No. 17 FAREWELL TO BELFAST.
DEPARTURE OF THE LARGEST VESSEL IN THE WORLD,
THE WHITE STAR LINER "TITANIC," 46,328 TONS, APRIL 3rd, 1912.

(Published by Walton, Belfast - Price band C)

Titanic had sixteen wooden lifeboats and four canvas collapsible lifeboats. This was the number of lifeboats which legally needed to be provided at that time.

It was based on overall tonnage of the vessel and surprisingly not on the number of people aboard. The lifeboats onboard were therefore only capable of carrying a maximum of 1167 people.

ARRIVAL AT SOUTHAMPTON

(Publisher unknown - Price band C)

Preparations for the maiden voyage were started on April 4th and this picture shows Titanic dressed in flags for the following day, Good Friday.

TITANIC DEPARTS SOUTHAMPTON

(Publisher unknown - Price band C)

During the early part of the year the coal miners had been on strike, this had ended on April 6th and Titanic would leave on April 10th.

It was not enough time for the newly mined coal to reach Titanic, and coal from other White Star and IMM ships in port plus leftover Olympic coal was used.

The strike had seen many of Southampton's seamen unemployed, and there was a rush to fill the vacancies aboard the brand new liner.

TITANIC DEPARTS SOUTHAMPTON

(Published by Rotary, pre-sinking postcard without disaster details - Price band B)

Just after 12 noon, with pilot George Bowyer aboard (pilot of the Olympic when she collided with HMS Hawke) the six tugs connected, the ship was slowly manoeuvred away from White Star's berth 44.

She began to glide forward towards the River Test. On the maiden voyage Titanic had a complement of 898 officers and crew aboard to operate the ship and look after some of the richest industrialists, bankers and families in the world.

TITANIC DEPARTS SOUTHAMPTON

(Published by E. W. M. - Price band C)

Among the passengers aboard were Mr. Bruce Ismay (White Star chairman), Mr. Thomas Andrews (Harland & Wolff Managing Director), and many very wealthy people.

Third class passengers were mostly comprised of émigrés to America including a large section of Scandinavians.

While nearly 100% of first class women and children would be saved, only 55% of women and 30% of children would survive from third class.

THE SS NEW YORK INCIDENT

(Publisher FGO Stuart, SS New York)

Titanic began to make her way down the dock towards where the liners New York and Oceanic were moored.

They were moored side by side as a result of the recent coal strike, and as Titanic's bow came along side the ropes holding New York snapped causing her to swing out.

Luckily with swift action from tug and Titanic a collision was averted, and only a slight delay of about an hour to the departure was caused.

TITANIC DEPARTS SOUTHAMPTON

(Published unknown, pre-sinking postcard - Price band B)

Captain Smith could now breathe a sigh of relief. It was to be his last voyage before retirement and a collision on the maiden voyage would have been a humiliating end to 25 years as a captain.

With his cheerfulness and easy nature he was a great favourite with the wealthy passengers aboard his ships.

PASSING RYDE PIER APRIL 10TH

(Published by Bekem Cowes, postally used April 19th 1912 3 days after the disaster illustrates how quickly some postcards were printed, issued and sold to satisfy the huge public response to the disaster - Price band C)

The voyage to Cherbourg continued uneventfully, and those aboard began to settle down for the seven day voyage to America.

The only concern was a small fire in one of the coal bunkers, probably started during loading in Belfast, and men were detailed to hose down and empty the bunker.

TITANIC ARRIVES AT CHERBOURG

(French card, publisher unknown, the postcard actually shows the Olympic labelled as Titanic - Price band B)

Because of the delay caused by the New York incident Titanic arrived at dusk.

Two specially built tenders the Nomadic and Traffic began transporting the mail, passengers and baggage, to and from the ship.

TITANIC ARRIVES AT CHERBOURG

(French card, publisher unknown, the postcard actually shows the Olympic labelled as Titanic - Price band B)

Among the joining passengers were many returning from the 'European' season. Fifteen first class and nine second class passengers disembarked at Cherbourg.

At 8pm the tenders returned to shore and Titanic set off to Queenstown, Ireland.

JOURNEY TO QUEENSTOWN

(Publisher unknown, shows Titanic at Cherbourg - Price band D)

At 11.30 am the next day (April 11th) Titanic arrived at Queenstown.

Anchored 2 miles offshore the tenders America and Ireland were sent to transport passengers, baggage and mail to and from the ship.

It was here that John Coffey, a stoker on board Titanic, deserted. It was believed he signed on to get free passage back to Queenstown.

STEAMING TO DISASTER

(Published by Walton, Belfast. This is a postcard published before the sinking and shows the Titanic arriving in New York, tugs and the statue of Liberty in the background - Price band B)

The ship was proving to be a great success with the passengers.

Many had commented on her steadiness and had taken advantage of the facilities, gymnasium, Turkish bath, swimming pool, squash court. Everyone had settled into a regular routine.

STEAMING TO DISASTER

(Publisher unknown, pre-sinking postcard to advertise the new liner - Price band B)

At 10.30 every day Captain Smith, dressed in full uniform with medals, would make his inspection of all parts of the ship.

After he would make his way to the bridge where he would check the ships progress, position, and read the various radio messages received.

All was proceeding well and the ship gradually increased speed to over 20 knots.

STEAMING TO DISASTER

(Published by Bekem, Cowes - Price band C)

The winter of 1912 had been mild causing ice flows to break away from the Arctic and drift south towards the normal shipping lanes.

On Sunday morning April 14th Cunarder SS Caronia reported 'bergs, growlers and field ice in 42 N 49 to 51 W' to Titanic. This was given to Captain Smith and posted on the bridge.

Top - RMS Lusitania (Cunard) the main competition to White Star

Bottom - SS Laurentic test bed for the reciprocating engines

Colour i

Top - Titanic & Olympic under construction H. & W. Belfast

Bottom - Colour interior of Olympic Verandah cafe

Top - Copyright J. Salmon Ltd., Sevenoaks, England ©

Bottom - Titanic postcard published by Tuck, UK

Top - SS Baltic one of the many ships who gave an 'ice ahead' warning

Bottom - SS Californian failed to see Titanic's distress flares

STEAMING TO DISASTER

(Published by E. Hopkin Southsea - Price band C)

Later in the afternoon White Star liner Baltic relayed to Titanic that "…Greek steamer Athinai reports passing icebergs and large quantities of field ice today 41 51' N 49 52' W…".

The message was delivered to Captain Smith while he was conversing with Bruce Ismay. The message was passed to Ismay who kept it, showing it to several passengers, before it was retrieved and posted on the bridge that evening.

STEAMING TO DISASTER

(Published by National, black and white printed card showing the White Star crest and disaster details - Price band A)

Evening was approaching and passengers started to notice the rapidly dropping temperatures. Slowly they left the decks for the warm interior rooms.

Further ice warnings were being overheard and relayed to the officers on the bridge.

STEAMING TO DISASTER

'THE TITANIC' S. S.; 882 ft. long; the largest boat in the world; sunk April 15, 1912, at 2:20 A. M.; on her maiden trip; with a loss of about 1,500 passengers.

(USA Published by Kraus N.Y. - Price band A)

It was after seven in the evening and Officer Murdoch ordered the forward hatches to be closed, to stop glow from the lights interfering with the ice watch from the crows nest.

The sea was flat calm and without the water ripples breaking on the bergs they would be hard to spot.

STEAMING TO DISASTER

(Colour postcard published by Tuck & Sons, Celebrated Liners #9898, postcard of Olympic labelled as Titanic - Price band B)

More messages of ice ahead were being received. It was 10 p.m. and Officer Murdoch was now in control of the bridge.

In the crows nest seamen Fleet and Lee had taken over the watch, and were instructed to be on the lookout for ice and growlers.

STEAMING TO DISASTER

(Copyright J.Salmon Ltd., Sevenoaks, England ©, from a water colour by W.Fred Mitchell - Price band A)

Just before 11.00 p.m. the freighter Californian sent the message that the ship was stopped and surrounded by ice. Before the Californian could finish the message Titanic's operator abruptly broke in "keep out! Shut up! You are jamming my signal......."

At the time he was busy relaying messages to Cape Race, Newfoundland. The Californians radio operator stopped his transmission and after a short time listening in to the Titanic's radio messages, turned off his station and went to bed.

STEAMING TO DISASTER

(Colour postcard published by Tuck & Sons, Celebrated Liners #9898-
Price band B)

It was around 11.30 p.m., the sky was cloudless and clear. In the distance was a slight mist, suddenly seaman Fleet gave the warning bell three sharp rings.

STEAMING TO DISASTER

(Published by Valentines UK, Titanic specifications and dimensions printed on the back - Price band A)

"Iceberg right ahead", "full speed astern", "hard a' starboard"[7] and the wheel was promptly spun as far as it would go. The switch to close the watertight doors was thrown.

Slowly the ship turned, enough to avoid a head on collision, and the iceberg slowly passed down the starboard side.

---

[7] It was later said that Titanic <u>may</u> have avoided the collision by going full speed ahead instead of full speed astern, because these large vessels turned more the faster they were going forward.

STEAMING TO DISASTER

(USA produced postcard, publisher unknown - Price band A)

At 11.40 p.m. the side of Titanic's hull scraped along the underwater iceberg causing a 300 ft long wound to her plating, ice fragments hitting the forward deck area.

DISASTER STRIKES

(German postcard publisher unknown - Price band B)

It had taken only 30 seconds from sighting the ice to the collision. Captain Smith rushed onto the bridge "What have we hit" he said "Iceberg Sir" Murdoch replied. The ship came to a halt.

The damage had crucially extended to the first six watertight compartments and as the ship was designed to survive any four forward compartments being flooded the ship was doomed.

DISASTER STRIKES

(Publisher unknown - Price band A)

Captain Smith and Thomas Andrews surveyed the damage[8] , it was grim news and they calculated the ship had only 1 ½ to 2 hours to live.

Officers and crew were roused and ordered to inform the passengers to assemble on the boat decks.

---

[8] The physical damage was probably only a few punctures each inches long and wide, but as the wound extended for such a long distance the ships fate was inevitable.

SOS TITANIC

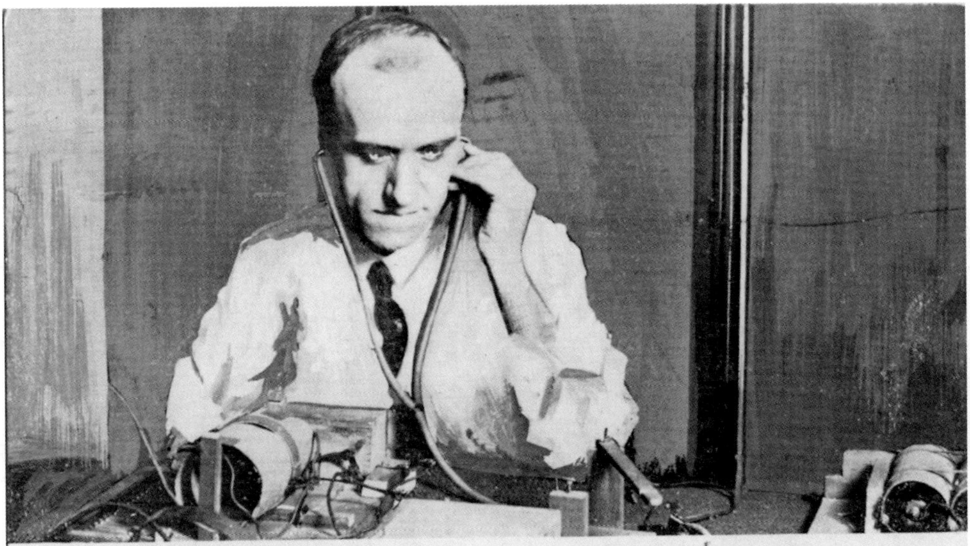

Wireless Operator Receiving Messages of Disaster

(USA published by F.A.Raphael Co, Chicago from a set of 12 - Price band B)

Officer Boxhall calculated the ships position to be 41 46' N, 50 14' W and at 12.25 am morse code message CQD (CQ for calling all ships and D for distress)[9] was broadcast.

The easier to broadcast SOS signal (three dots, three dashes and three dots again) had just been introduced and later the wireless operators Bride and Phillips would use this signal. One of the first times it had been used in an emergency.

[9] The ships position was hastily calculated and incorrect by four miles south, six miles east. CQD was more commonly known as 'Come Quickly, Distress'

THE SINKING OF TITANIC

(Publisher unknown - Price band A)

At 12.45 the first of the lifeboats was lowered.

Many of the passengers refused to believe this fine ship was doomed and the danger they were in. Not enough lifeboats were aboard and Captain Smith (who went down with the ship) ordered women and children first.

The first lifeboat was lowered with only 28 of the capacity of 65 aboard.

THE SINKING OF TITANIC

(Published by Pictorial Stationery Co. - Price band A)

Distress rockets were being fired at regular intervals to attract the attention of a vessel whose lights were seen from the bridgc.

The vessel whose lights could be seen may have been the Californian and her Captain Stanley Lord would become the centre of controversy as they were accused of ignoring Titanic's plight.

THE SINKING OF TITANIC

(German published by Oskar Stoltze Hamburg - Price band B)

On board the situation was getting worse and now boats were being lowered with a full complement.

THE SINKING OF TITANIC

(USA published by White Star N.Y. - Price band B)

As the angle of the ship increased loose fittings started to break free and smash, many passengers began the fruitless climb to the stern of the ship.

Suddenly the lights aboard went out and she slid into the ocean. It was reported that the stern ‘rose vertically in the air and hung there for a few seconds’ before plunging 12000 feet to the sea floor.

It was 2.20 am and the violence of the last few moments was replaced by a strange calm, disturbed only by the survivors in the water who would later die of hypothermia in the icy water.

CARPATHIA TO THE RESCUE

The Carpathia—Rescued 705 of the Ill Fated Titanic's Passengers

(USA published by Raphael Co. Chicago from a set of 12 - Price band B)

The Carpathia was approximately fifty-eight miles away and acknowledged the Titanic's distress message steaming hard to reach her as quickly as possible. She arrived at Titanic's distress point at about 3.30 am.

Lifeboat No 2 was the first to be spotted, and slowly the others began rowing towards the lights of Carpathia.

CARPATHIA TO THE RESCUE

(USA published by Raphael Co. Chicago from a set of 12 - Price band B)

The second boat to reach Carpathia was boat No 1 with only a dozen occupants. It had taken about four hours to rescue all those who had survived the disaster.

CARPATHIA TO THE RESCUE

(USA published by Joseph Koehler N.Y. - Price band A)

With all the survivors aboard a crowd still scanned the sea hoping to see their loved ones who had been left behind, but without any success.

At 8.50 am Carpathia set sail, eventually bringing the survivors to New York on Thursday April 18th.

Of the 2228 passengers and crew who had set sail aboard Titanic only 705 had survived and 1523 had perished in the cold waters of the North Atlantic.

NEWS OF THE TRAGEDY

Copyright by Underwood & Underwood, N. Y.
Group of "Titanic's" Rescued Passengers on Deck of the "Carpathia"

(USA published by Raphael Co. Chicago from a set of 12, showing a group of rescued passengers aboard Carpathia - Price band B)

The news gripped the world and special editions were printed over the following days as more information about the passengers and ship arrived.

On both sides of the Atlantic White Stars offices were besieged by people wanting more information. Slowly the enormity of the disaster was filtering through.

At the Cunard pier 54, almost 40,000 people awaited the arrival of Carpathia.

BANDMASTER WALLACE HARTLEY

(Publisher unknown - Price band B)

Among the many heroes aboard the Titanic were the ships band, who all perished in the disaster. They were:

Top: J. Clarke (bass), J.Woodward (cello), Percy Taylor (piano), George Krins (violin)

Middle: J.Hume (violin), Wallace Hartley (bandmaster), W.Brailey (piano)

Bottom: R.Bricoux

The band continued playing ragtime and other cheerful tunes, while the Titanic sank, reportedly finishing with the Hymn 'Nearer my god to thee'.

BANDMASTER WALLACE HARTLEY

(USA published by Tichnor Bros. - Price band A)

Wallace Hartley was born in Colne, Lancashire. He made about 80 voyages on liners before joining the Titanic as bandmaster.

It was two weeks after the sinking that his body was eventually recovered by cable ship Mackay-Bennett.

He was still wearing his bandsman uniform and strapped to his chest was his music box. His body was returned to Colne on the ship SS Arabic.

THE AFTERMATH

(Colour postcard publisher unknown)

Most surviving members of Titanic crew were returned to England aboard Lapland after giving evidence to the US inquiry.

It had been one of the worst disasters in history and soon many questions were being asked. In both Britain and America inquiries were set up almost immediately to discover the cause of the disaster and the lessons to be learnt.

THE AFTERMATH

(USA Publisher unknown - Price band A)

One of the immediate effects of the inquiries was to increase the number of lifeboats to cover all passengers and crew aboard any ship.

MEMORIAM POSTCARDS

(Published by National UK - Price band A)

Many postcard publishers started to produce memorial postcards for the disaster to satisfy the huge appetite for anything Titanic.

This card, edged in black to show mourning, showing inset portrait of Captain Smith, Titanic and some ship details plus a verse of 'Nearer my god to thee'.

MEMORIAM POSTCARDS

(French published - Price band A.)

Memoriam postcards for the disaster were published throughout the world, as the news of the terrible disaster spread.

This French postcard, showing inset the Titanic and some ship details plus 4 verses of 'Nearer my god to thee' in English and French.

The music to the hymn was reportedly the last played by the band as the ship went down.

MEMORIAM POSTCARDS

(Published by E.A.Bragg, Falmouth, showing Titanic, Captain Smith and wireless operator John Phillips - Price band B)

Senior of the radio operators was John “Jack” Phillips. He relieved his junior operator Harold Bride, and staying at his post broadcasting CQD and later SOS almost until the ship sank.

Harold Bride survived with severely frost-bitten feet, after clambering aboard one of the collapsible lifeboats in the last minutes of the sinking.

MEMORIAM POSTCARDS

(Published by National - Price band A)

The words and music to 'Nearer my god to thee' were to appear regularly on the memoriam cards.

MEMORIAM POSTCARDS

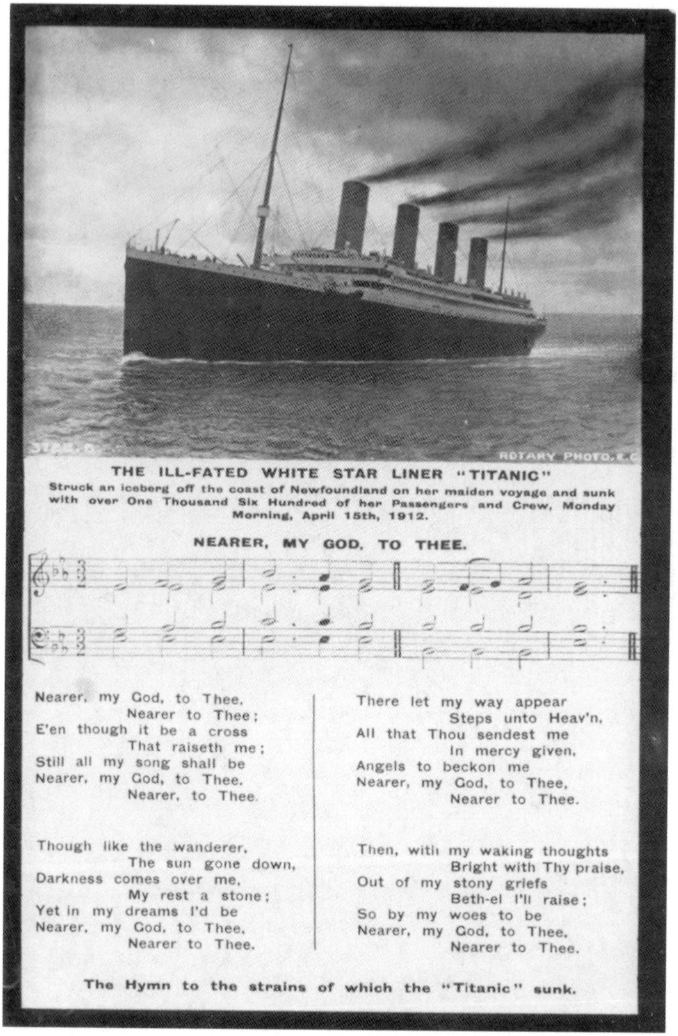

(Published by Rotary Photographic Series - Price band A)

A retouched image, smoke has been added and can be seen coming from all 4 funnels, which was not possible as the last funnel was used for ventilation.

BAMFORTH MEMORIAM POSTCARDS

(Published by Bamforth & Company Series No 21 - Price band A)

This set of six cards were produced in two distinctive shades. The more common are black and white and the less common are dark sepia and white.

(Published by Bamforth & Company Series No 22 - Price band A)

The Titanic sinks and Jesus appears on the cross. The postcards were very popular and sold well to a public very interested in the loss of the ship.

BAMFORTH MEMORIAM POSTCARDS

(Published by Bamforth & Company Ltd, Holmfirth [England] and New York Series No 23 - Price band A)

The Bamforth cards were produced in a set of 6 showing a combination of the Titanic sinking, words and music to the hymn and a grieving woman.

The hymn was written by Arthur Sullivan and bandmaster Wallace Hartley had said he would have liked it to be played at his funeral.

(Published by Bamforth & Company Ltd, Holmfirth [England] and New York Series No 24 - Price band A)

The best postcard in the set of 6 shows the Titanic sinking and lifeboats in the water.

(Published by Bamforth & Company Ltd, Holmfirth [England] and New York Series No 25 - Price band A)

Although 'Nearer my god to thee' was thought to be the last hymn played some survivors reported hearing the hymn 'Autumn' during the last moments.

BAMFORTH MEMORIAM POSTCARDS

(Published by Bamforth & Company Ltd, Holmfirth [England] and New York Series No 26 - Price band A)

Postcard shows Titanic sinking and angels appearing on the staircase to heaven.

CAPTAIN SMITH MEMORIAM

(Publisher unknown, the reported last words 'Be British' printed at the bottom - Price band C)

This was to be Captain Smith's last voyage and a fitting end to a 25 year career. He was a great favourite amongst the wealthy passengers.

REMEMBERING THOSE WHO DIED

(Published by Dixon, Colne UK - Price band A)

The grave and headstone of bandmaster Wallace Hartley 1879-1912. He was buried in his home town of Colne with full honours, and about 40,000 people lined the route as the mile long procession made its way to the cemetery.

REMEMBERING THOSE WHO DIED

(Published by Tierneys Liverpool - Price band A)

Monument erected at Liverpool dedicated to the Engineers who died on the Titanic.

REMEMBERING THOSE WHO DIED

(Publisher unknown - Price band A)

Monument erected at Belfast in memorial to the men who died on the Titanic, inscribed with some disaster details.

REMEMBERING THOSE WHO DIED

(Publisher unknown, showing a stone and plaque dedicated to Engineer Arthur Ward erected by his fellow townsfolk and friends - Price band A)

Money was raised all over the country and plaques and statues erected to commemorate those who had died.

REMEMBERING THOSE WHO DIED

(Publisher unknown - Price band B)

In Southampton's East Park a permanent memorial was erected to the engineers who perished on the Titanic.

Southampton had suffered badly with many families affected by the loss of relatives and loved ones.

It was unveiled two years after the disaster and attended by a crowd of 100,000 and is a permanent reminder of the loss of engineering crew aboard Titanic.

DISCOVERY OF THE WRECK SITE

(Published by G.Clarke, Dorset showing support vessel Knorr)

As the technology of dead water exploration advanced many expeditions had tried to find the wreck of Titanic. In 1985 the French IFREMER organisation and the Woods Hole Oceanographic Institution launched a joint expedition to find Titanic.

Robert Ballard, aboard research vessel Knorr, was reaching the end of the attempt to find the wreck. The search area had been based on where Carpathia had recovered the lifeboats and the reported position from Titanic as she sank.

DISCOVERY OF THE WRECK SITE

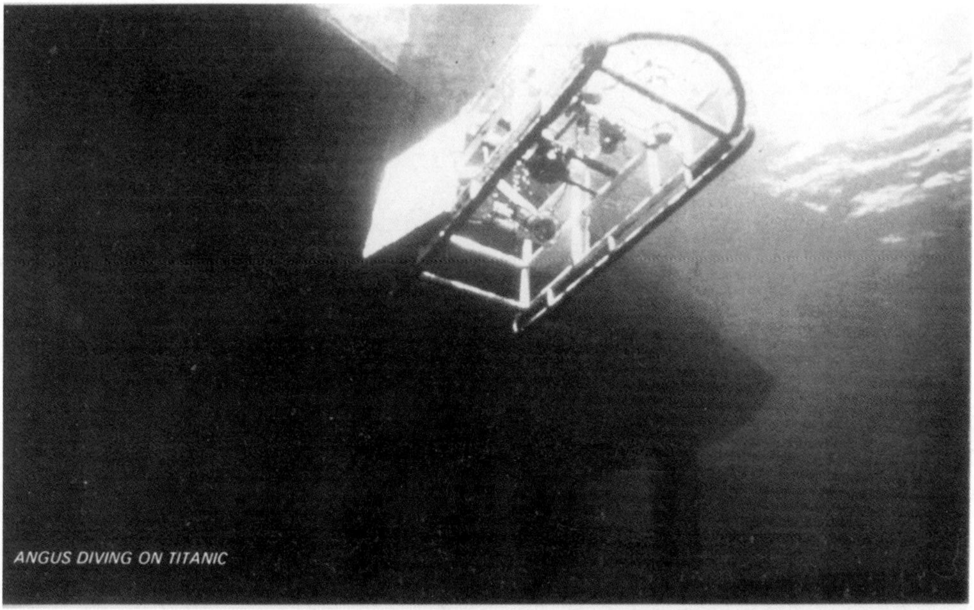

(Published by G.Clarke, Dorset showing acoustic search vessel ANGUS)

Ballard had decided to abandon the sonar search and launched submersible Argo with its camera to search for the debris field of the wreck.

The ship as it sank would have deposited a large debris field on the sea bed and it was thought it would be easier to find this than the comparatively small wreck itself.

DISCOVERY OF THE WRECK SITE

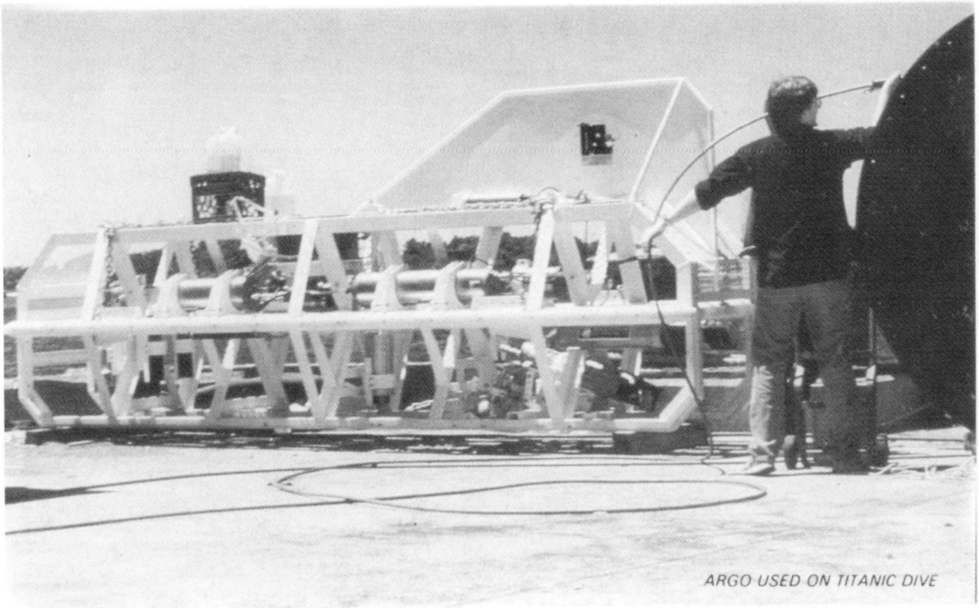

(Published by G.Clarke, Dorset showing submersible Argo)

Argo would "fly" 20-40 meters above the seabed sending live video back to Knorr via a strong coax cable and using powerful underwater lights.

It was after days of tedious searching that the first glimpse of Titanics boiler appeared on Argos monitor.

The French co-leader of the expedition Jean-Louis Michel summoned Robert Ballard and with high emotions both celebrated the discovery of the Titanic, over two miles down on the sea bed.

DISCOVERY OF THE WRECK SITE

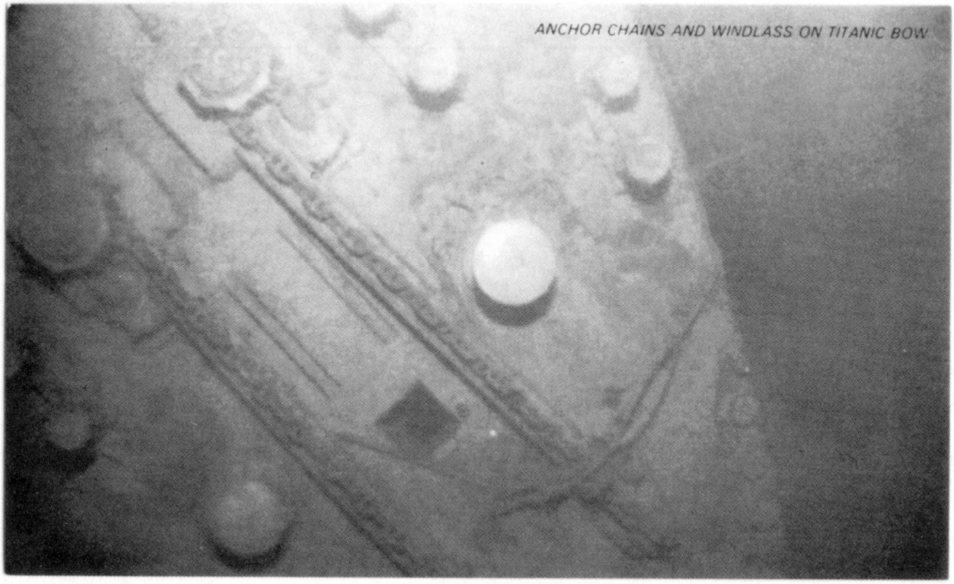

(Published by G.Clarke, Dorset showing Titanics anchor chains)

These black and white images were some of the first pictures to be released to the eager public awaiting news of the wreck.

The US and French teams that had collaborated on the discovery were to 'fall out' over the film and video rights of the discovery.

After news of the wrecks discovery many people came forward with schemes to raise or salvage the wreck and items for commercial museums etc.

DISCOVERY OF THE WRECK SITE

(Published by G.Clarke, Dorset)

The postcard shows the remains of the After crane lying on the sea bed amongst the debris.

The US House of Representatives passed a bill to make the wreck site a memorial and to provide for reasonable research, exploration and salvage if appropriate in an attempt to stop the plundering, for financial gain, of what is a grave.

DISCOVERY OF THE WRECK SITE

(Published by G.Clarke, Dorset)

Postcard showing the port and starboard cranes.

Subsequent expeditions were to photograph and film the wreck in greater detail, and some salvage of artefacts from the debris field was undertaken.

DISCOVERY OF THE WRECK SITE

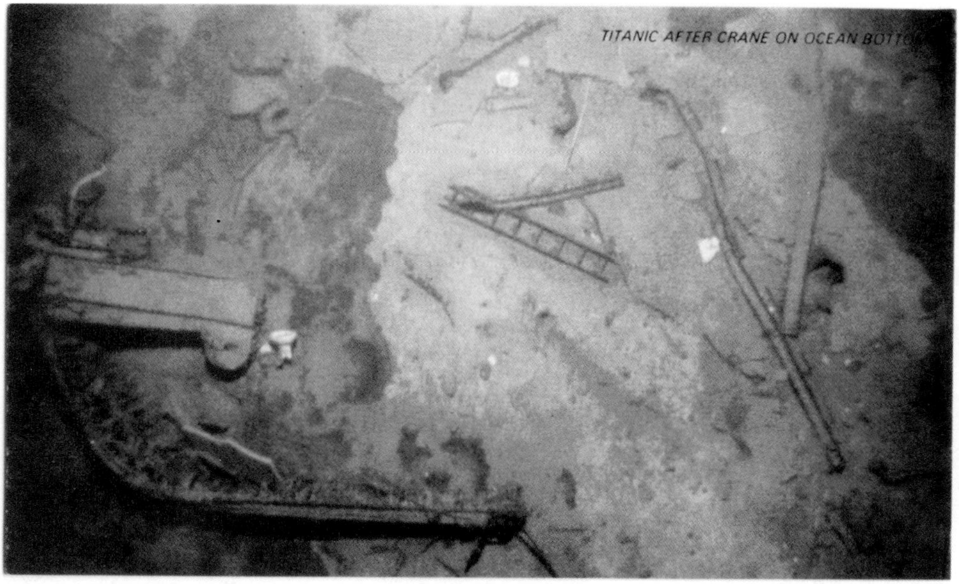

(Published by G.Clarke, Dorset showing After crane in debris field)

Whether the wreck should be left alone or researched in detail is a personal opinion, but many interesting facts and knowledge have been gained by studying the wreck.

One certain fact is that the iron of the wreck is slowly being turned to rust and scientists predict the whole hull will eventually rust away to dust and disappear for ever.

THE DIFFERENCE BETWEEN TITANIC AND OLYMPIC EXPLAINED

<u>GUIDE TO TITANIC POSTCARD PRICES</u>

It is difficult to give a complete guide to Titanic cards prices without producing a catalogue which is beyond the scope of this book. With the volume of different cards available and the scarcity of some of the cards it is unlikely that such a catalogue will ever be produced. This guide is meant as a BRIEF GENERAL guide to prices and what to look for when purchasing Titanic postcards.

Pre-sinking cards are generally more difficult to find, as until the Titanic disaster it was just another ship. The Olympic had grabbed all the initial attention as the first ship to be launched.

Memoriam postcards are more popular in the UK than the USA, were produced in many different designs and do not fetch the highest prices. They were produced within days of the disaster and many feature real photographs of the Olympic, as contemporary photographs of the Titanic itself were not available to the postcard publishers.

Postally used cards add a small premium to the price as the postmark on the back is useful in ascertaining an approximate date the card was produced.

I have included a price guide to the cards illustrated in this book in 4 bands:

- <u>BAND A</u> - for postcards that are some of the commonest in the UK and USA. These are usually printed and not real photographic and are some of the first cards any collector will purchase to start their collection. They are easily available at fairs and via the internet and at the time of writing are valued up to £100 or $150.

- <u>BAND B</u> - these are the cards that can be found quite regularly and are usually real photographic ‘Olympic’ pictures used to illustrate the ‘Titanic’ and the more unusual printed cards or related subjects. At the time of writing these are valued at £100 to £300 or $150 to $450.

GUIDE TO TITANIC POSTCARD PRICES

- BAND C - this band includes the interesting real photographic Titanic which usually is only offered occasionally and are difficult to find. At the time of writing these are valued at £300 to £500 or $450 to $750.

- BAND D - this band is for the rarer cards which are not easy to find and are seldom offered. It is the price band that is hardest to implement as demand will drive some of the prices very high indeed. The cards to look out for are the unusual real photographic Titanic, anchors, associated machinery, fitting out, postally used on board Titanic, Titanic silk postcard, and unusual associated events (i.e. funerals, provisions for the voyage etc.). The prices for these cards is totally dependent on their scarcity and start at £500 or $750 and can fetch unpredictable high prices, driven by demand, for the very rare cards.

To view Titanic postcards currently for sale visit - www.anmb.co.uk

ACKNOWLEDGEMENTS

The author would like to thank the following without whom this book would not have been possible:

The Bamforth Postcard Collection, Leeds, UK for their kind permission to reproduce the set of six 'Bamforth Memoriam' postcards.

J. Salmon Ltd., Sevenoaks, England.

R. Terrell Wright, USA.

Mark Chatterton

and Gordon Clarke, for all their help.

While every effort has been made to trace and acknowledge all copyright holders, I would like to apologise should there be any errors or omissions.